Poems about
Choices

Raintree is an imprint of Capstone Global Library Limited, a company incorporated in England and Wales having its registered office at 7 Pilgrim Street, London, EC4V 6LB – Registered company number: 6695582

www.raintreepublishers.co.uk
myorders@raintreepublishers.co.uk

Text © Capstone Global Library Limited 2014
First published in hardback in 2014
Paperback edition first published in 2015
The moral rights of the proprietor have been asserted.

Produced for Raintree by
White-Thomson Publishing
www.wtpub.co.uk
+44 (0)843 208 7460

Edited by Sonya Newland
Cover design by Tim Mayer
Designed by Ian Winton
Concept design by Alix Wood
Production by Victoria Fitzgerald
Originated by Capstone Global Library Ltd
Printed and bound in China

ISBN 978 1 4062 7292 5 (hardback)
17 16 15 14 13
10 9 8 7 6 5 4 3 2 1

ISBN 978 1 4062 7299 4 (paperback)
18 17 16 15 14
10 9 8 7 6 5 4 3 2 1

British Library Cataloguing in Publication Data
A full catalogue record for this book is available from the British Library.

Poems reproduced by permission of:
p. 9 "The Road Not Taken" taken from *The Poetry of Robert Frost* edited by Edward Connery Latham. Published by Jonathan Cape. Reprinted by permission of The Random House Group Limited.
p. 25 "Catrin" by Gillian Clarke, from *Selected Poems* (1985) Reproduced by permission of Carcanet Press Limited.
p. 30 "Southern History" from NATIVE GUARD: Poems by Natasha Trethewey. Copyright © 2006 by Natasha Trethewey. Reprinted by permission of Houghton Miffflin Company. All rights reserved.
p. 41 Nikki Giovanni, "Choices". Copyright © 1978. Reprinted by permission of the author.

Picture credits can be found on page 63.

Every effort has been made to contact copyright holders of any material reproduced in this book. Any omissions will be rectified in subsequent printings if notice is given to the publisher.

Disclaimer
All the internet addresses (URLs) given in this book were valid at the time of going to press. However, due to the dynamic nature of the internet, some addresses may have changed, or sites may have changed or ceased to exist since publication. While the author and publisher regret any inconvenience this may cause readers, no responsibility for any such changes can be accepted by either the author or the publisher.

CONTENTS

Experiencing poetry about choices

The old pond—
A frog jumps in,
The sound of water.

The eleven words of this poem – just three short lines – are an invitation to experience poetry. The pond and the frog were first brought to mind by a poet called Bashō, who composed the lines in the 17th century. The words describe a simple scene, but it is clear that Bashō chose each image with great care.

The original poem appeared in Japanese; this is one of several popular translations. Countless people have read a version of these lines before you, yet no two people have experienced this small poem – a **haiku** – in exactly the same way. Some readers picture a frog in their minds long after reading about it. Others might imagine the splash. What does this haiku make you think?

SPIRIT OF HAIKU

Haiku is a form of poetry that originated in Japan. A modern haiku has three lines, with five syllables in the first and last lines, and seven syllables in the middle. The challenge for those writing haiku is to craft a striking message that appeals to the senses in just 17 syllables. A classic haiku takes nature as its subject. The ideas are always stated in plain language, with no rhymes, **similes**, or **metaphors**.

Similes are **figures of speech** that compare two things using words such as "like", "as", "if", or "than". Example: "Bashō's haiku is *like* a text message from long ago."

Metaphors are figures of speech that link two things by carrying some aspect of one thing to another. Example: "His *words* are an *open window*."

Searching for meaning

Poetry is all about choices – for the poet and for the reader. The experience of poetry can help people sharpen their senses. Sharing poems like this can also help people understand each other better.

A poem delivers a message, or central meaning, in lines of **verse**. But each reader chooses his or her own way of reading a poem. You might just scan the lines for meaning. Perhaps you read aloud, or under your breath. Maybe you prefer to let the words ripple in your mind. Even a simple poem like this haiku contains a complex mix of elements. We each perceive those elements our own way.

Think about this
Symbols of change

In stories, frogs are often **symbols** of change because during their life cycle they go through processes in which they change their shape. They start as eggs, become tadpoles, and then develop into full-grown frogs. Can you think of any other creatures that might be considered symbols of change due to their life's journey?

Shape and meaning

In ordinary writing, or **prose**, one string of words follows another across a page. The lines form blocks of text, and breaks appear between paragraphs. Poetry is different. Poets can structure poems in any way they like. A finished poem might look like a ladder of lines, or the words might be placed to form a pattern that looks like lace. Sometimes, the poet's message appears in the first lines and the rest of the poem supports the central idea. More often, a reader needs to take the poem apart in order to find the meaning.

The arrangement of seeds in a sunflower might seem random, but the seeds form spirals in a regular sequence. Just like in nature, there is often a hidden meaning or logic to poems.

TYPES OF POEMS

A **narrative poem** tells a story. To find its main ideas, you can read the entire text and then summarize what happens. A **lyric poem** has a different structure, but you can approach it in a similar manner. Instead of telling a story, a lyric poem explores emotions in a songlike way. After reading a lyric poem, you can try to **paraphrase** the main thought in different words.

Back to Bashō

Your first idea about a poem will often lead to other ideas. For example, you might summarize Bashō's haiku this way: *A frog decides to jump in water*. This summary could lead to other questions:

- *A frog decides...* Do frogs really make choices the way that people do?
- *...to jump in water*. What water, and why?

These questions may make you return to the poem. You might notice that it does not mention *deciding* – the only action word that appears is *jumps*. The poet suggests something about a jump made by a frog. A better summary might be: *A frog makes a splash*. On reading the poem again, you may see that Bashō does not state that the sound of water is a splash. The images of a frog and a pond suggest certain sights, sounds, smells, and even the memory of what standing water feels like. But this is all the poet gives us. His central idea seems to be the impression his words make, and the way this emphasizes what is and is not happening.

BASHŌ
1644–1694
Born: Iga Province, Japan

Bashō's birth name was Matsuo Kinsaku. As a child, he was a servant. In the home where he worked, he learned to create **collaborative poems** – those written by more than one person – called *renga*. Later, he became known as a teacher of poetry. He made several long journeys and wrote about his experiences. Today, he is considered the master of haiku and is known by the single name Bashō. His poems are carved on monuments throughout Japan.

Bashō remains widely celebrated in Japan more than 300 years after his death.

Did you know? Bashō took his name from the Japanese word for "banana tree".

"The Road Not Taken"

What are your favourite song lyrics? Why do you like them? Do the words of the song affect your emotions or sum up how you feel sometimes? Do they affect the way you think about the world?

Songwriters, rappers, and other poets choose their words carefully, because they know that great songs and strong poems are powerful. Writing poetry is a way of giving everyday words a deeper meaning, and of connecting many different people with one another.

By selecting words with care, a writer also chooses the **tone** (the attitude) that readers hear, see, and feel in the writing. In poetry, it is possible to outline strange dreams, strong emotions, and spiritual awareness. These are things that many people find difficult to discuss.

Finding the way

Each writer has a reason for writing. The subject of a poem can be as simple as a feeling or as momentous as an event that changes history. In "The Road Not Taken", Robert Frost takes a simple, everyday moment and fills it with meaning. Read the poem and write down your first impressions in a notebook. Take note of any questions that come up.

Think about this
Larger ideas

Narrative poems often describe a very specific event as a way of referring to much larger ideas or issues. On one level, Frost's poem is about taking a walk in the woods, but there is much more to it than this. At what point in the poem do you realize that there is more going on than outdoor exercise?

"The Road Not Taken"

by Robert Frost

Two roads diverged in a yellow wood,
And sorry I could not travel both
And be one traveler, long I stood
And looked down one as far as I could
To where it bent in the undergrowth;

Then took the other, as just as fair,
And having perhaps the better claim,
Because it was grassy and wanted wear;
Though as for that the passing there
Had worn them really about the same,

And both that morning equally lay
In leaves no step had trodden black.
Oh, I marked the first for another day!
Yet knowing how way leads on to way,
I doubted if I should ever come back.

I shall be telling this with a sigh
Somewhere ages and ages hence:
Two roads diverged in a wood, and I—
I took the one less traveled by,
And that has made all the difference.

The poem's story

In a poem with a plot, it helps to **summarize** the action. What is happening and where? Lines of poetry do not necessarily look like regular sentences, but they function in similar ways. Most often, the lines of poems have a subject, and the subject does or thinks about something. In "The Road Not Taken", someone goes walking in the woods and comes upon two paths. The walker chooses the less-travelled path, and wonders what this will come to mean in the end.

Your summary should also answer the question "When?" Look for details that reveal the timing of the walk. The wood is yellow, which suggests autumn, and this is supported by the fact that there are leaves covering the pathways. Autumn is often used as a symbol of change in literature.

Summarizing the action can lead to a more difficult question: "Why?" The author's reason for writing is often a reflection of his or her purpose. But sometimes the poet starts writing with one idea in mind and ends up altering it. We are left to work out the purpose ourselves.

It seems clear that in "The Road Not Taken" there is more going on than a simple walk in the woods. Very often, poets use natural settings as a way to speak about larger ideas, or themes. Writers use nature to show lessons about life. In this poem, the speaker is sharing feelings about decisions and indecision. The poem captures these complicated feelings in a memorable manner.

Analysing structure

In addition to outlining the facts in a poem, it is helpful to approach the text as if it were a painting. First, **survey** the poem. See how long it is; look at how its lines are arranged. For example, "The Road Not Taken" has a clear structure. It has four **stanzas** (groups of lines), each containing five lines.

THE FIVE Ws

One basic tool for taking a poem apart is using the five Ws: *Who, What, Where, When,* and *Why.* Look for the details that fall into each category. Start by identifying the speaker or **narrator**. In Frost's poem, the speaker is "I". Keep in mind that poets and other storytellers often speak through characters. The speaker could be the poet, or it could be a character that the poet is using to get across his or her meaning.

Next, read "The Road Not Taken" out loud. Go slowly. Don't worry whether you are saying the words in the "right way" or whether you are going to be able to make the poem rhyme. The poet has done this work for you. All you need to do is to allow the words to fall into place on their own.

Pay attention to the punctuation. When a line ends without a punctuation mark, this means you should keep reading. Move quickly to the next line. When a poet uses a full stop, it signals that you need to pause briefly at that point.

Think about how the poem sounds. For example, do words echo one another? In this case, the first, third, and fourth lines rhyme. The second and fifth lines also rhyme. Now, what do you think is the purpose of each stanza?

Mapping out the meaning

In your notes, you might want to sketch four boxes, one for each stanza. Then write down what happens in each stanza. For example, in this poem, the narrator describes a choice in the first stanza and makes a decision in the second. In the third, he begins to show remorse, and looks to the future and a larger meaning in the fourth.

TAKING NOTES

If something is not easy to understand or causes you to wonder, make a note of it. Write down words that you do not know. Look for **context** clues (the words before and after the unknown word) that might reveal its meaning. For example, you may not understand the word "diverged", but there is a clue to its meaning in the next line – "And sorry I could not travel both". To diverge is to move in different directions from a starting point.

Getting the message

One way of discovering even more meaning in a poem is to find out when it was written. "The Road Not Taken" was published in 1915 in a magazine called *The Atlantic Monthly*. Frost was a young man at the time. He sometimes told people that he wrote this poem with a friend – Edward Thomas – in mind. When the two men went walking together, Thomas would often express regret that they had walked one way rather than another.

You could say that this particular poem is about an indecisive friend of Frost's. You could say that Frost wrote the poem to tease his friend, and you would be right. However, there is more to the story. An American by birth, Frost and his wife and children had been living in the United Kingdom and had just returned to the United States. They planned to live on a farm while Frost tried to sell his poems. He was at a point in his life when his choices were going to shape his family's future, and it is choices that are the theme of this poem.

Choices present people with "what ifs" on many different levels. Wearing one pair of shoes rather than another can make it harder to rush from place to place. Choosing to ignore a problem with a friend may lead to a fight later. Deciding to be in a good mood can make a difference throughout the day.

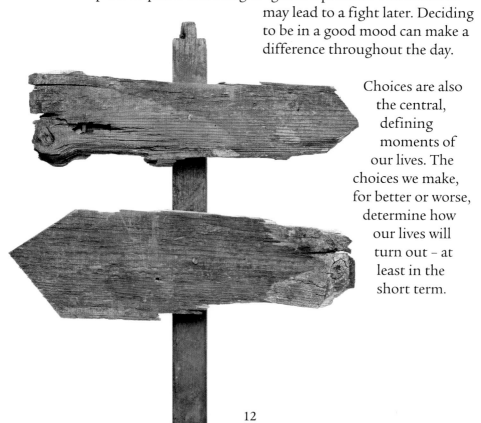

Choices are also the central, defining moments of our lives. The choices we make, for better or worse, determine how our lives will turn out – at least in the short term.

ROBERT FROST

1874–1963

Born: San Francisco, California, USA

This photo shows Robert Frost on his farm in 1942, many years after he had made his own choices about becoming a writer and a farmer.

After his father died in 1885, **Robert Frost**'s family moved from California to Massachusetts to be with his mother's parents. He attended both Dartmouth and Harvard universities for a few years before becoming a teacher, author, and farmer. Frost was awarded the Pulitzer Prize for poetry four times – in 1924, 1931, 1937, and 1943.

Did you know? In the 1967 novel by S. E. Hinton, *The Outsiders*, the lead character Ponyboy recites the poem "Nothing Gold Can Stay", by Robert Frost.

Experience reflected in verse

One of the most fascinating things about language is how people rarely say anything the same way twice. Even when an individual poet returns to the same subject matter, the way he or she presents that subject usually changes. The meaning will have been altered by the poet's experiences in life.

Throughout his life, Frost wrote poems about moments of thoughtfulness and indecision. In one, the speaker is in a kitchen, watching the wind blow the trees back and forth outside. The speaker feels called to leave – to vanish – but instead chooses to stay at home. In another, the speaker is travelling at night in a horse-drawn carriage on a snowy road. The speaker stops to look at the snow-filled woods and enters a dreamy state. Awakened by the shaking of the horse's bells, the speaker decides to keep moving.

A choice moment

Frost wrote poems about picking apples, watching ice melt, finding flowers in fields, listening to wind, and gazing at stars. He wrote about common, ordinary experiences, but he presented these ideas and images as something in which people could feel and hear something more: the power of his creative insights. When you read Frost's poems, he is inviting you to make connections of thought and feeling along the same lines. Poetry is ordinary language that a poet has arranged so a deeper meaning can break out. Poems mimic those moments when something special occurs and you feel a new awareness.

In appreciation

Have you ever experienced a moment when something as simple as a falling feather or the shine of broken glass caused time to seem to slow down? Or have you ever suddenly seen an everyday object in a new and different way? Perhaps there are curtains you pay little attention to, but they cast a certain shadow and you have a sudden memory of trying to capture shadows when you were very young. When reading "The Road Not Taken" – or any other poem – look for images, words, or phrases that transport you somewhere else, drawing your attention into a fuller experience of life.

POINT, EVIDENCE, EXPLAIN (P.E.E.)

To help you analyse poetry, you can use a method known as Point, Evidence, Explain (P.E.E.):

Point. Comment on one aspect of the poem. For example: "The speaker seems to be facing an important choice."

Evidence. Quote from the poem to back up your point: "The speaker says, *Two roads diverged in a wood, and I— / I took the one less traveled by, / And that has made all the difference.*"

Explain. Give greater detail to explain your point: "These lines come at the end of the poem. By this point, the speaker has come upon two paths and has decided which path to take. The narrator is thinking forward to a day when he will be looking back at this moment and what it ended up meaning. In these lines, the poet repeats the word *I*. This seems to emphasize that this decision will affect the speaker in important ways, and the speaker is very aware of that fact."

Recording your impressions

Taking notes while reading poetry can sharpen your awareness, and this is a skill that can be applied to more than just analysing poems. Review the main questions to ask yourself.

Who? The "Who?" is usually the speaker of the poem – the **persona**. However, the question can also relate to other characters. In "The Road Not Taken", the speaker is alone on a walk in the woods. In many other poems that you encounter, there may be several characters who interact with one another. In some poems, you may find that the existence of other people is simply implied.

What? This is the way that events occur, also thought of as the situation or circumstances. When reading a poem, look closely at the way that it opens, as this can give vital clues about the "What?"

Where? The **setting** is the place where the action or feeling occurs in a piece of writing. This is the time and place, which poets use to draw their readers into their imaginary worlds.

When? Look at the order in which events present themselves. This is the way that the past, present, and future are represented. The easiest plots to follow are those that follow a **chronological order**, the order of time. In Frost's poem, events appear chronologically, but writers do not always feel bound by this logic.

Why? When asked to explain the meaning behind his poems, Frost once said: "If I wanted you to know I'd have told you in the poem." He uses **understatement** and ordinary moments to point to larger concerns, but he does not necessarily map out their meaning.

If there were a sixth *W* it might stand for "Wonder". What Frost does *not* tell you is also important. Where is the speaker going? Why is he alone? It is as if the poet wants you to **speculate** about the next part of the story.

Think about this
In conflict

In addition to figuring out the five Ws, you can also pry open a poem by identifying the conflicts it illustrates. In "The Road Not Taken", the speaker is experiencing self-doubt. The main conflict is what it feels like to be at odds with oneself, wondering what to do or decide. Can you think of a time in your own life when a choice led you to greater opportunities? Has a choice ever set you on a challenging path?

"The Charge of the Light Brigade"

Poems can depict small scenes and world events. Many poems explore the internal struggles that people experience in everyday situations, as in Frost's "The Road Not Taken". However, a poem may also take as its subject a much larger conflict. "The Charge of the Light Brigade" by Alfred, Lord Tennyson is a good example of this.

As you read the poem, note down your first impressions and record unfamiliar words or concepts, along with your best guess as to their meaning. With older poems in particular, it can help your understanding if you map out as much of the meaning as you can to begin with, then go back and re-read the details you missed the first time.

This famous painting by Richard Caton Woodville Jr is just one of many that depicts the famous charge. It presents the cavalrymen in heroic pose.

"The Charge of the Light Brigade"

by Alfred, Lord Tennyson

Half a league, half a league,
   Half a league onward,
All in the valley of Death
   Rode the six hundred.
"Forward, the Light Brigade!
"Charge for the guns!" he said:
Into the valley of Death
   Rode the six hundred.

"Forward, the Light Brigade!"
Was there a man dismay'd?
Not tho' the soldier knew
   Someone had blunder'd:
Theirs not to make reply,
Theirs not to reason why,
Theirs but to do and die:
Into the valley of Death
   Rode the six hundred.

Cannon to right of them,
Cannon to left of them,
Cannon in front of them
   Volley'd and thunder'd;
Storm'd at with shot and shell,
Boldly they rode and well,
Into the jaws of Death,
Into the mouth of Hell
   Rode the six hundred.

Flash'd all their sabres bare,
Flash'd as they turn'd in air,
Sabring the gunners there,
Charging an army, while
   All the world wonder'd:
Plunged in the battery-smoke
Right thro' the line they broke;
Cossack and Russian
Reel'd from the sabre stroke
   Shatter'd and sunder'd.
Then they rode back, but not
   Not the six hundred.

Cannon to right of them,
Cannon to left of them,
Cannon behind them
   Volley'd and thunder'd;
Storm'd at with shot and shell,
While horse and hero fell,
They that had fought so well
Came thro' the jaws of Death
Back from the mouth of Hell,
All that was left of them,
   Left of six hundred.

When can their glory fade?
O the wild charge they made!
   All the world wonder'd.
Honour the charge they made!
Honour the Light Brigade,
   Noble six hundred!

WORDS YOU MAY NOT KNOW

Sabring: this means using sabres – a kind of sword.
Cossack: a Cossack was the name given to certain people from Ukraine and parts of Russia, especially a soldier from those places who rode a horse into battle.

Telling the tale

This poem was first published in 1870. Poems like this, from a long time ago, may seem foreign at first. However, you can use the same tools to help you understand poetry from any period.

Begin by summarizing the poem. Here, for example, you can say that 600 soldiers ride into battle – and certain death ("Theirs but to do or die"). Almost immediately, the subject raises questions for many modern readers. Who are "the six hundred" who choose to die for their cause? Who chose to send them into battle? What is their cause?

History in action

Allusions are references to things beyond the text you are reading, such as historical events or other works of literature. With older poems, such as "The Charge of the Light Brigade", it helps to know something about these allusions.

In this poem, Tennyson was writing about the Battle of Balaclava, which took place during the Crimean War (1853–1856). The British were fighting the Russians in the Crimea (now Ukraine). At Balaclava, more than 600 soldiers in the British **cavalry** were given the wrong orders to charge at a battery of Russian cannons. The Russians were positioned on the higher ground of the valley and gunned them down as they charged.

ALFRED, LORD TENNYSON

1809–1892

Born: Somersby, Lincolnshire, England

Alfred, Lord Tennyson began writing poetry when he was a teenager. He and two of his older brothers published their first collection of poetry when Alfred was only 17.

In 1850, Queen Victoria named Tennyson as the nation's official poet. In this role of **Poet Laureate**, it was Tennyson's job to mark celebrations and other important matters of history with his writing.

Did you know? Tennyson's name was Alfred Tennyson. Alfred, Lord Tennyson is just a formal way of showing that he had been made a lord.

Tennyson was Britain's Poet Laureate — the poet appointed to write poems for official occasions — when he penned "The Charge of the Light Brigade".

INSIDE OUT

Conflict can be external or internal. In external conflicts, one character may fight another. A character or a group of characters may struggle against the ways of society. Or characters may fight against nature or even machines. In internal conflicts, a character may struggle to be a better person. In both cases, the **resolution** of the conflict is the way that it all works out.

Knowing the background

The Crimean War was one of the first wars fought after the invention of trains and telegraphs. News of the deaths travelled faster than before. It is said that Tennyson wrote the poem after reading about the battle in a newspaper. The poem itself was first published in a newspaper. Publicly criticizing the people who were responsible for such disasters was a new experience – a new choice – for people like Tennyson:

> *Not tho' the soldier knew*
> *Someone had blunder'd:*

This photograph shows the battlefield at Balaclava, looking towards the Russian artillery positions just out of sight in the distance. Compare it to the painting on page 18.

THE IMPACT OF THE INDUSTRIAL REVOLUTION

Tennyson was writing during the later years of the **Industrial Revolution**. With machines doing more of the labour, more people found time to examine their thoughts. Printed materials, in which people shared ideas and knowledge, were becoming widespread. The rise of the machine also placed nature in a new light. Suddenly, humans seemed more powerful – capable of fighting nature.

Patterns of sound

The shape of the poem is like a river of words, pouring from top to bottom. The lines are all quite short. You can see that words repeat at the start of a number of the stanzas, including "Half", "Forward", "Theirs", "Cannon", "Into", "Flash'd", and "Honour".

A number of words that would normally end in the **suffix** -ed are instead given an apostrophe followed by the letter d. The overall effect is to make the writing appear especially active. It is as if the poem were relaying a message so pressing that there is not enough time to speak.

Tennyson repeats many lines, and the effect of this is a kind of drumbeat. This helps a reader feel the rush and heat of the battle. Sounds also repeat – for example, the hiss in "Storm'd at with shot and shell". Read the poem aloud, and you can hear the whizzing gunshots and cannon fire. The structure of the poem is tidy, but the words boom and break across the page.

When reading this poem, you may also notice that the words do not fall into the pattern of regular speaking or sentences:

Theirs not to reason why,
Theirs but to do and die:

Highly stylized wording often appears in older, classic poetry, which called for specific patterns of rhythm and rhyme.

Language in the poem

Tennyson speaks of the "valley of Death", which refers to a verse in the Bible that is often read at funerals. He also writes about the "jaws of Death" and the "mouth of Hell". He **personifies** death, giving it human features.

You may also see words in this poem that you do not fully understand, such as "league". In Tennyson's day, a league was a unit of measurement equal to about 5 kilometres (3 miles). By the line "Half a league onward", you may have realized that a league was a measure of the land ahead.

"Catrin"

The poem "Catrin" by Gillian Clarke captures a small but highly emotional moment between two people. Like "The Charge of the Light Brigade", it tells the story of a battle. However, unlike the large, public setting of Tennyson's great fight, "Catrin" is a narrative that describes a struggle and a choice that take place on a small stage.

The basic facts

There is a narrator in this poem ("I") who is talking about another character – someone with long, brown hair and a "rosy, / Defiant glare". The speaker addresses the other character as "you", a fact that connects this character with the title of the poem. Catrin is the name of the girl who is asking to skate for one more hour. This is a simple summary of the poem, but reading it closely and analysing the images it contains will reveal much more.

"Catrin"

by Gillian Clarke

I can remember you, child,
As I stood in a hot, white
Room at the window watching
The people and cars taking
Turn at the traffic lights.
I can remember you, our first
Fierce confrontation, the tight
Red rope of love which we both
Fought over. It was a square
Environmental blank, disinfected
Of paintings or toys. I wrote
All over the walls with my
Words, coloured the clean squares
With the wild, tender circles
Of our struggle to become
Separate. We want, we shouted,
To be two, to be ourselves.

Neither won nor lost the struggle
In the glass tank clouded with feelings
Which changed us both. Still I am fighting
You off, as you stand there
With your straight, strong, long
Brown hair and your rosy,
Defiant glare, bringing up
From the heart's pool that old rope,
Tightening about my life,
Trailing love and conflict,
As you ask may you skate
In the dark, for one more hour.

WORDS OF CONTRADICTION

The poet uses figures of speech to connect words that
seem **contradictory**, such as "wild, tender circles" and
"love and conflict". These are **oxymorons**: figures of
speech that help illustrate the way that opposite feelings
can rise up at the same time.

Picture it

In "Catrin", the speaker and the skater are in conflict, and it seems clear that the speaker is in charge of the skater. Little by little, you may sense that the speaker is the skater's mother. The mother must choose whether or not to let her daughter go out in the dark, but this decision seems to stand for something much larger.

Here is one way to examine the **imagery**. The poem begins in a "hot, white room". The room has a window. The speaker stares out at passing cars and changing traffic lights. This seems to illustrate the passing moments, the pressure building inside the room – and some kind of turning point. Inside, everything is hot and white, or clean and blank. The reader can feel the emotion building.

A "tight / Red rope of love" ties the characters together. This suggests the umbilical cord – the cord that connects a mother and child at birth. If so, the "hot, white / Room" more clearly appears as a hospital room. The rope becomes a metaphor for the relationship between these two characters: they cannot seem to break free from each other.

Metaphors in the poem

The image of the rope appears again in the second stanza.
This time, it is "tightening" around the speaker's life, and she
describes it as "Trailing love and conflict". The daughter is asking
to be allowed to skate in the dark – she wants an adult's privileges
– and the mother feels a rush of emotion in response. Part of her
wants her daughter to stay tied to her and their home.

In the second stanza, Clarke describes a "glass tank clouded with
feelings". The last mention of glass was in the windows of the
white room. Now, the glass is clouded, and the defined space
is more like a fish tank. These lines invite you to look into this
space the way that you might look into a fish tank. The speaker
is also looking in, remembering something that happened in the
past, searching for meaning. The fish tank could be an image
from the hospital nursery. It could be many things, depending
on the background of the reader.

Think about this
Autobiography

The poem "Catrin" is **autobiographical**. Autobiography is a
story of a writer's own life, as told by the writer themselves.
Biography is also a story about a particular person's life,
but the writer is not the subject of the story. How do you think
biography and autobiography might differ in their approaches to
telling a story or recounting an event in the life of the subject?

Patterns in the poem

"Catrin" deals with two conflicts – an external conflict between two people and the internal conflict that the speaker feels. The line lengths are irregular, which conveys a sense of these struggles. The words are not formed with even beats, and they are held together by a number of **half rhymes**. For example, the words "first" and "tight" share a final consonant. The effect of this becomes clear when reading the lines aloud, feeling how and where the vowels and consonants fall.

The poet repeats the words "I can remember" and "to be". In the first stanza, words with the suffix *–ing* repeat as **end rhymes** of the last syllable. Although very little matches in **adjacent** lines, a few patterns do show up. The words "square" and "squares" echo each other, for example. "Lights" and "tight" also echo each other. Why do you think the poet makes these choices?

Between the lines

Open form poetry like "Catrin" asks a lot of its readers. It still uses rhythm and rhyme, but the pattern is less obvious than in other types of poetry. Open form poems often do not have regular punctuation at the end of lines. Instead, the poets use the space around the text to

signal when to start and stop, and they often place punctuation within the lines. The effect is that some phrases roll into the white space, such as when "people and cars taking" breaks to the next line, "Turn at the traffic lights". The words "taking", "turn", and "traffic" are harsh, like tapping or rapping on a window.

When vowels or vowel sounds repeat in words in connecting phrases, it is called **assonance**. In "Red rope of love which we both", the consonants repeat, but so do vowels within the words. By controlling the way her readers hear her words, the poet affects the tone, the meaning, and the interpretation of the poem.

GILLIAN CLARKE

1937–

Born: Cardiff, Wales

Gillian Clarke was a teacher of language arts who turned to writing and lecturing. In 2008, she was given the post of National Poet of Wales by Literature Wales, a sponsor of literature-related projects. She often visits schools, giving poetry readings to students who are studying her poems.

Did you know? Clarke says that she wrote the poem "Catrin" to answer this question: "Why did my beautiful baby have to become a teenager?"

Clarke has received several awards for her work, including the Queen's Gold Medal for Poetry in 2010.

RHYME AND REPETITION

Rhyme is a repetition of sound. It is easiest to detect at the end of lines. There are different types of rhymes:

- **Perfect rhyme** occurs when sounds repeat in the last syllable (brigade/dismay'd).
- **Imperfect rhyme** or **near rhyme** occurs when sounds almost rhyme, such as when sounds repeat on stressed and unstressed syllables (child/white).
- Half rhyme occurs when final consonant sounds repeat (up/rope).

In addition, look within lines for assonance (matching vowels), **consonance** (matching consonants), and **alliteration** (matching first consonants).

"Southern History"

The tone of "Catrin" is very personal and emotional – a mother writing about her daughter. The close relationships between family members lend themselves to this treatment. Poets also reach for words that convey truth about important matters affecting all of society. Natasha Trethewey's poem "Southern History", which deals with the issue of racism, is an example of this.

"Southern History"

by Natasha Trethewey

Before the war, they were happy, he said,
quoting our textbook. (This was senior-year

history class.) *The slaves were clothed, fed,
and better off under a master's care.*

I watched the words blur on the page. No one
raised a hand, disagreed. Not even me.

It was late; we still had Reconstruction
to cover before the test, and – luckily –

three hours of watching *Gone with the Wind.*
History, the teacher said, *of the old South –*

a true account of how things were back then.
On screen a slave stood big as life: big mouth,

bucked eyes, our textbook's grinning proof – a lie
my teacher guarded. Silent, so did I.

A summary of the poem

This short poem is written in open verse. There are seven stanzas, each with just two lines. As well as the usual commas and full stops, the text is punctuated by **parentheses** and dashes. Some words are **italicized**.

There are several characters in the poem. The two main characters are the narrator ("I") and a male teacher, identified by the **pronoun** "he". The italicized words are mainly those spoken by the teacher. The other characters are the students in the classroom, who do not speak or act, and a slave – also silent – who appears in a film.

The poem describes a history lesson, in which students are watching the movie *Gone with the Wind*. The film is a romance set in the southern states during the American Civil War, when the North fought the South over issues of slavery and states' rights. After years of brutal fighting, the South was in ruins. The government freed the slaves on the **plantations**, and the main characters had to adjust to a new life.

NATASHA TRETHEWEY

1966–
Born: Gulfport, Mississippi, USA

Natasha Trethewey grew up in New Orleans, Louisiana, and Atlanta, Georgia. Her third book of poetry, *Native Guard*, won the 2007 Pulitzer Prize for poetry. In 2012, she became the 19th US Poet Laureate.

Did you know?
Trethewey turned to writing poetry after her mother was shot and killed by her stepfather.

Trethewey is fascinated by the Civil War, and the event appears in several of her works.

31

History and truth

What happens in this poem? The teacher tells his students that slaves were happy before the war because they were fed and cared for by their masters. The speaker of the poem implies that she or he knows this is not true. Perhaps other students in the classroom also know that the teacher's words are untrue. History is supposed to record the facts about the past, but no one speaks up to contradict the teacher. The poem illustrates a choice to stay silent in the face of lies.

Choosing to stay silent

In a wider sense, the poem also reflects an ongoing struggle to fit into a less-than-perfect society. Most people understand what it feels like to hear a person saying things the listener knows to be false or ignorant. In these cases, you must choose whether to confront that person or let it go. This can be a difficult decision, especially if you feel pressure to fit in with your peers and to go along with what is happening.

In "Southern History", Trethewey describes the circumstances in a very matter-of-fact tone – she reports events as a news reporter might. By treating the subject matter in this way, the poet allows readers to make their own judgements about the situation.

Points of view

The narrator tries to disconnect from feelings as a way to get through the lesson. Yet feelings seep through in the middle and at the end of the poem. The words blur on the page, suggesting that he or she may be too angry or emotional to see straight – or may even be crying.

BY ASSOCIATION

When analysing poetry, look for the **denotation** and **connotation** of the words. Denotation is the dictionary definition of a word – for example, as a verb the word "blur" means "smear". Connotation is the set of ideas associated with a word. Connotations include personal connections that the poet or the reader bring to the word. They also include cultural associations that most people can see in the poet's word choice. The connotations of the word "blur" relate to tears and strong emotions.

The poem is told from the narrator's **point of view**. However, the teacher is in control of the classroom, and his view dominates. The reader sees through the narrator's eyes when the words blur on the page. Readers can feel the speaker's discomfort by reading between the lines. By the end, when the "lie" is called out, the reader already has a sense of what the narrator feels about the situation.

Think about this
"Not even me"

The words "Not even me" emphasize the choice the narrator makes to stay silent. They also suggest that the speaker knows better than the history books. The final lines "a lie / my teacher guarded. Silent, so did I" confirm this. Why? What circumstances might make the narrator feel that he or she knows more? Finding out a bit about Natasha Trethewey may give you some ideas.

This painting shows slaves working on a cotton plantation in Mississippi in the 1800s.

"A Crown of Sonnets Dedicated to Love"

Poets arrange sounds the way musicians do. When people talk about music or poetry, they use similar descriptions. There are lines of music and lines in poems. There are stanzas in both as well.

Musicians can often "hear" the notes when looking at a sheet of paper. The ability to read rhythm and rhyme in poetry happens in much the same way. The more time you spend reading and enjoying poetry, the easier it becomes to "hear" the rhythms and pick out the patterns of rhyme.

Lyric poetry

Lyric poetry is much like songs presented by solo performers. In a lyric poem, the words sound musical. The poet's purpose in writing is to share feelings and observations about life through a single narrator.

To explore these ideas, read and take notes on this **sonnet** from a longer work called "A Crown of Sonnets Dedicated to Love". The poet, Lady Mary Wroth, lived in the late 16th and early 17th centuries. She wrote in an older form of English, which can present some challenges for a modern reader. However, the subject matter is relevant today, and the tools you use to understand modern poems work on older ones in the same way. Wroth writes about love, and about choosing to move forward with a difficult relationship.

LAST AND FIRST LINES

A "crown" is a form of sonnet in which the last line of one sonnet is used as the first line of the next sonnet. So the next sonnet in this series begins with the line "Is to leave all, and take the threed of Love".

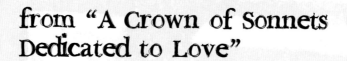

from "A Crown of Sonnets Dedicated to Love"

by Lady Mary Wroth

In this strange Labyrinth how shall I turne,
Wayes are on all sids while the way I misse:
If to the right hand, there, in love I burne,
Let mee goe forward, therein danger is.
If to the left, suspition hinders blisse;
Let mee turne back, shame cryes I ought returne:
Nor faint, though crosses my fortunes kiss,
Stand still is harder, allthough sure to mourne.
Thus let mee take the right, or left hand way,
Goe forward, or stand still, or back retire:
I must these doubts indure without allay
Or helpe, but trauell finde for my best hire.
Yet that which most my troubled sense doth move,
Is to leave all, and take the threed of Love.

WORDS YOU MAY NOT KNOW

Although Wroth does not use complicated words in her sonnet,
she uses old-fashioned spellings that can make some words hard
to recognize. For example, "sids" = sides; "suspition" = suspicion;
"indure" = endure; "trauell" = travel; and "threed" = thread. Different
spellings for these and other words are used in different versions of the
poem, too. Sometimes letters were added, such as in "Yett" and "lett".
In other versions, letters were dropped from the end of words, such as
using "strang" instead of "strange" in the first line.

The labyrinth

Frost wrote about choosing a particular fork in a road. Wroth wrote about choosing a path through a maze. In ancient Greek **mythology**, a "labyrinth" was a maze that held the Minotaur, a creature that was half man and half bull. We still use the word today to mean a maze.

In medieval Europe, various communities built another kind of labyrinth. These were more like paths outlined on the ground than mazes with walls. In many cases, a patch of pavement in or around churches featured a spiral path that people were supposed to follow on their knees while praying. Wroth's "Labyrinth" of "Love" has these connotations, too.

This ancient mosaic was designed in the pattern of a labyrinth. In the centre is a picture of the Minotaur being defeated.

Metre in the poem

Copying out the poem using modern English spellings can reveal the strong sense of **metre** in this sonnet. Metre is the pattern of rhythm found in the lines of a poem, arising from the way the words are spoken. Words are made up of syllables, and in each word some syllables are **stressed** while others are unstressed.

Study the first line of the sonnet and listen for the stressed syllables: "In *this* strange *Labyrinth* how *shall* I *turne*." The stress falls on every other syllable, in a pattern a bit like a heartbeat: duh-DUH, duh-DUH, duh-DUH, duh-DUH, duh-DUH. Now, look further. The pattern repeats in every line.

End rhymes and half rhymes

Sonnets are highly structured poems, marked by end rhymes and the regular beat of the syllables. In this sonnet, "turn" rhymes with "burn" and "return". The word "bliss" rhymes with "kiss". These are perfect rhymes, in which the sounds match almost exactly. The end rhymes strike chords the way that music does.

The poem also uses half rhymes. The word "is" is not exactly in tune with "bliss" or "kiss", but they half rhyme. Likewise, the word "move" is a half rhyme with the word "Love". There are **internal rhymes** as well. These are the echoes within lines that carry the poem along and suggest that words are flowing.

LADY MARY WROTH
1587–1653
Born: England

Lady Mary Wroth was born Mary Sidney. Her father was Sir Robert Sidney, an earl in Elizabethan England. Wroth's love life was complicated for a woman of her time. After her husband, Sir Robert Wroth, died she was linked romantically with William Herbert, the powerful Earl of Pembroke, and she had two sons with him.

Did you know? Lady Mary Wroth was the first Englishwoman to publish a work of fiction. Called *The Countesse of Mountgomeries Urania*, it described the adventures and romances of two women.

Getting technical

Sonnet writing is a form of wordplay. The writers of sonnets often tried to say something witty in a formal way. The rules for sonnet writing have varied by place and time, but a classic English sonnet has 14 lines. Often the lines appear in a rhythm known as **iambic pentameter**.

The duh-DUH sound of the unstressed and stressed syllables is a unit of rhythm called an iamb **foot**. Each line has a certain number of feet, and metre is the pattern of these feet. Wroth's sonnet is written in iambic pentameter. In this type of verse, each line is made up of five iamb feet (the duh-DUH sound repeats five times).

READING THE METRE

The term "iambic pentameter" comes from the kind of feet being used and the number of feet that appear. To see why it makes sense, consider the four most common feet used in English poetry:

anapest   duh-duh-DUH
dactyl   DUH-duh-duh
iamb   duh-DUH
trochee   DUH-duh

Each line of a poem can be divided into a number of feet:

A line with one foot is in *mono*meter.
A line with two feet is in *di*meter.
A line with three feet is in *tri*meter.
A line with four feet is in *tetra*meter.
A line with five feet is in *penta*meter.

So iambic *penta*meter is a line that has *five* feet of the *iamb* (duh-DUH) sound. *Penta* is the Greek **prefix** for "five".

The most famous sonnet writer is William Shakespeare, who penned more than 150 of these verses on many different themes.

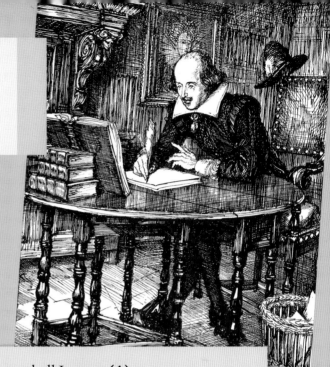

Rhyming ways

Sonnets follow a rule of rhyme as well. The stanzas keep to a regular pattern of end rhymes, as shown here:

In this strange Labyrinth how shall I turne, **(A)**
Wayes are on all sids while the way I misse: **(B)**
If to the right hand, there, in love I burne, **(A)**
Let mee goe forward, therein danger is. **(B)**
If to the left, suspition hinders blisse; **(B)**
Let mee turne back, shame cryes I ought returne: **(A)**
Nor faint, though crosses my fortunes kiss, **(B)**
Stand still is harder, allthough sure to mourne. **(A)**
Thus let mee take the right, or left hand way, **(C)**
Goe forward, or stand still, or back retire **(D)**
I must these doubts indure without allay **(C)**
Or helpe, but trauell finde for my best hire. **(D)**
Yet that which most my troubled sense doth move, **(E)**
Is to leave all, and take the threed of Love. **(E)**

William Shakespeare usually followed the rhyming pattern ABAB, CDCD, EFEF, GG. The sonnet by Wroth incorporates BABA instead of CDCD, for a similar effect.

BALLADS

Ballads are closely linked to lyric poetry. Ballads are narrative poems made for singing. They have simple stanzas and often feature a **refrain**, which is a stanza that repeats.

"Choices"

By the time Wroth wrote her crown of sonnets, that particular form of poetry was past the height of its popularity. Today's poets draw from a wide range of poetic forms, but they still look to and appreciate older forms such as sonnets. Poetry is like music that way: different styles arise in certain time periods, but then stick around, influencing later forms of poetry.

A modern poem may not always seem to have been written to an obvious set of rules like a sonnet, but look closer. Examine the way that the poem appears. Look at Nikki Giovanni's poem "Choices" and consider what its shape seems to say.

The shape of things

If you compare Giovanni's poem with Wroth's sonnet, the newer poem may appear less organized. In fact, a great deal of thought has gone into the presentation of both pieces. Giovanni manages the readers' reactions just as Wroth does. Some words repeat, and some sounds suggest light rhyme. The line breaks are chosen carefully, because each one is a signal.

"Choices" has five uneven stanzas. The shortest is just two lines plus one word long. The longest is nine lines long. Modern poets may not stick to certain metres, but they continue to work with the lengths of lines. They understand that the way the words appear affects the tone of the poem and its message. They pay attention to the **visual rhythm** of the words.

MUSICAL INFLUENCES

Jazz music became popular in the 1920s. At a jazz set, listeners expect to hear sounds that swing – and that surprise them. Rap started to gain followers in the 1970s. Fans of rap expect to hear chanting and a heavy beat. Both these forms of music are now well established and they influence each other. New artists are coming up with ways to use them both.

"Choices"

by Nikki Giovanni

if i can't do
what i want to do
then my job is to not
do what i don't want
to do

it's not the same thing
but it's the best i can
do

if i can't have
what i want   then
my job is to want
what i've got
and be satisfied
that at least there
is something more
to want

since i can't go
where i need
to go   then i must   go
where the signs point
though always understanding
parallel movement
isn't lateral

when i can't express
what i really feel
i practice feeling
what i can express
and none of it is equal
i know
but that's why mankind
alone among the animals
learns to cry

Think about this
Visual poetry

The ancient Greeks wrote poems in shapes such as those that resembled eggs or wings. In Wroth's time, some poets were writing poems in similar shapes. Throughout the 20th century, poets experimented with **concrete poetry**, in which the shape suggests the poem's subject. Some poets are still exploring the possibilities of visual poetry today. When writing your own poetry, think about what shape it could take to reflect its subject matter.

Asking questions

To find the meaning of "Choices", you can begin by asking questions. The speaker in "Choices" is "I", and in this case, the "i" is small rather than a capital letter. Why has the poet made this choice to go against common practice in writing? To **infer** the meaning of the small "i" you might ask why the speaker sees himself or herself as "lowercase". Do the small letters suggest that the narrator is feeling small and humble?

The lack of capital letters is a deliberate choice by the poet. The use of "holes" is another – places where words fail and open spaces signal that thoughts are trailing off. On two occasions, the pause comes before the word "then". Why? Perhaps this is because the speaker is discussing failure. This is a poem about dealing with disappointments, and the holes in the lines seem to represent the struggle this involves.

Who am I?

Why does each lowercase "i" follow another down the middle of the poem, much like falling tears? Why are there no commas or full stops, just spaces to show silence or the omission of material within the line? Each line just ends, with no special mark. Does the speaker simply lack the energy to make them?

Open verse like Giovanni's "Choices" leaves much of the meaning of the poem in the control of the reader. It leads a reader to question each choice the poet made in his or her writing.

Seeing the picture

In this poem, Giovanni works with concepts rather than imagery. There is no frog, no pond, no woodland path. The speaker is talking about wants, jobs, doing, satisfaction, signs, movement, expression, and feeling. These concepts do not paint pictures.

The narrator is showing what it feels like when choices are limited. The two words that repeat most are "do" and "go". These verbs are very simple, and it is hard to think of any words that better illustrate the outcomes of basic choices. People often struggle with whether to do something or go somewhere.

The speaker is also talking about an inability to express feelings. The poem itself seems to show how people suppress their emotions. The entire poem builds up to the last word: "cry".

NIKKI GIOVANNI

1943–

Born: Knoxville, Tennessee, USA

Nikki Giovanni was born Yolande Cornelia Giovanni. She grew up in Ohio. A famous poet and non-fiction writer, Giovanni is also recognized for her work as a civil rights activist and college professor. She has written and edited numerous books of poetry.

Did you know? In 2004, Giovanni was nominated for a Grammy Award for Best Spoken Word Album.

Many of Giovanni's poems focus on teaching children African American history and dealing with the social issues facing black youth.

"Love, Poem 1: Choice"

The poems in this book cover a range of choices that people must make, from which path to take in life to whether to stand up to ignorance. In "Love, Poem 1: Choice", Emily Dickinson at first seems to be talking about the person she has chosen to be her partner. But it soon becomes clear that the main idea is something else entirely.

"Love, Poem 1: Choice"

by Emily Dickinson

Of all the souls that stand create
I have elected one.
When sense from spirit files away,
And subterfuge is done;

When that which is and that which was
Apart, intrinsic, stand,
And this brief tragedy of flesh
Is shifted like a sand;

When figures show their royal front
And mists are carved away, —
Behold the atom I preferred
To all the lists of clay!

WORDS YOU MAY NOT KNOW

intrinsic: this means belonging to the nature of a thing.
subterfuge: a subterfuge is a deception.

Personal acceptance

As you read the poem, you may realize that it is about Dickinson's acceptance of herself, and the contentment that flows from that acceptance. In the first stanza, the poet refers to a belief that she has chosen her own soul. The second stanza establishes the difference between life as we know it and some kind of afterlife. The third stanza emphasizes what was said before.

Rhyme and metre

Try reading the poem aloud. Strong end rhymes appear in the second and fourth lines of all three stanzas. Consonants echo throughout. There is a hiss that comes from the use of the letter *s*. The second stanza is filled with *th* and *f* and *ph* sounds. The final lines mix these sounds. This suggests patterns that are coming loose.

By comparison, the metre is under strict control. By tapping it out on a table, you can see: "duh-DUH, duh-DUH, duh-DUH, duh-DUH / duh-DUH, duh-DUH, duh-DUH". This is the same metre as in certain hymns. What might this reveal about both the poet and the poem?

IN HER WORDS

Emily Dickinson used words such as "clay" and "atom" in inventive ways. Scholars who study her poems have created a special website called the Emily Dickinson **Lexicon** to explain the connotations she gave to words. For example, it explains the word "clay" as:

> *Earth; soil; basic elements; earthly part of human body; material of the human body (Genesis 2:7); human body as distinguished from the spirit.*

In Dickinson's day, people did not fully understand atoms. They knew that everything was made of tiny building blocks. But few people could imagine the smaller parts that existed inside these particles. When you search for her use of the word "atom", you find a long list of uses, including:

> *First principle of matter; individual in a physical, tangible, material state; [wordplay] Adam; man; first human being according to the Bible.*

Weighty words

Dickinson uses words that may be unfamiliar to you, such as "subterfuge". If so, look at the words around it. When discussing subterfuge, the poet is talking about her soul or spirit. She appears to be suggesting something about a life beyond this one – that subterfuge does not exist if her senses and her spirit part ways. The prefix *sub* is Latin for "under". From these clues, you can guess that subterfuge is beneath something. In fact, the word means "deception". It is something hidden.

Even after deciphering some words, questions may remain unanswered. The speaker is discussing spirits and atoms, but related words and ideas end up in an unexpected order. For example, in the line "When sense from spirit files away" we would expect to read *"flies* away". Dickinson's phrasing is unusual – sometimes even strange.

EMILY DICKINSON

1830–1886

Born: Amherst, Massachusetts, USA

Emily Dickinson grew up in a wealthy, well-known family in Massachusetts. As she became older, Dickinson had trouble with her eyes and she stayed inside more and more. Some people have suggested that she had an illness that kept her from socializing, but others believe that Dickinson lived alone so she could dedicate herself to her poetry. Her writing reveals a deeply **introspective** soul, who was very perceptive about the world around her.

Emily Dickinson never aspired to be a well-known poet. In fact, she did not even intend her poetry to be published.

Did you know? Emily Dickinson wrote her poems on scraps of paper, such as the backs of recipes. The poems often take their metre from the rhythms of hymns.

Layers of meaning

Much like Giovanni does in "Choices", Dickinson uses concepts rather than imagery. This means that the few words that denote objects stand out: "flesh", "sand", "mists", "atom", and "clay". Of these, only three of them are things that a person can touch.

The poem may make Christian readers think of the Bible. The Book of Genesis describes the creation of the world, and includes a phrase that is often reflected in poems: "for dust you are and unto dust you shall return". This is a warning that God gives people before sending them into the world. Dust is a part of sand and clay.

In the Book of Genesis, God creates the first man, Adam, out of the "dust of the ground".

The poet's life

Dickinson began writing in earnest when she was a teenager, and over the course of her life she wrote nearly 1,800 poems. The United States was a relatively young country at the time. The first state universities were being established, and US scholars were coming into their own.

It was at this same time that Noah Webster was putting together the first dictionary of American English – different from British English. Dickinson studied his list and responded to it with words of her own. She played with language, symbols, and allusions. Those who knew her said that she used her dictionary the way that other people use holy books.

Emily Dickinson's house in Amherst, Massachusetts. In later life, she rarely left her home, communicating with friends and family mainly by letter.

DICKINSON'S PHILOSOPHY

Working in relative isolation, Dickinson seemed to write with a fever. "If I read a book [and] it makes my whole body so cold no fire can warm me I know that is poetry," she told Thomas Wentworth Higginson, who would eventually publish her poems. "If I feel physically as if the top of my head were taken off, I know that is poetry. These are the only ways I know it. Is there any other way?"

Understanding the context

How does some understanding of Dickinson's life affect your reading of "Love, Poem 1: Choice"? The narrator calls life a "brief tragedy of flesh", as if already connected to something greater. This is a clue that can help you unlock some of the stranger turns of phrase. For example, who or what are the figures showing their "royal fronts"? Are they people such as kings and queens? Does the word "fronts" refer to the fronts in which people line up for battle? Perhaps Dickinson was picturing people lined up to meet their maker, trying to appear a certain way.

When is it that mists are carved away? In life, it is the sunshine of day that cuts through a morning mist. If this is part of her meaning, what kind of morning does she refer to? Is it any given morning? Or does it refer to a specific morning – perhaps at the end of time? These images seem to refer to Dickinson's idea of what happens to everyone eventually, even though this link is not made explicit.

What do you think Dickinson was saying? In the end, the point of taking apart a poem is putting it back together. Each time you do, you choose the meaning you take away from it – and you understand more just by trying.

Think about this
In time of war

Dickinson wrote many of her poems during the years of the American Civil War. How do you think that living in those times might have affected her? Can you imagine being alive when your country is involved in such a bitter and violent internal struggle?

Putting it all together

Achoice is a moment rich with meaning. In "The Road Not Taken", the narrator commits to one path and then sadly says: "I shall be telling this with a sigh / Somewhere ages and ages hence". He is saying that making a choice also means giving up opportunities that might have followed from taking a different path.

Can you think of some of the choices you made – for better or for worse? Did some lead to good things, while others represent lost opportunities? Maybe you had to choose between two sports. Or maybe you had to pick one of two classes because they met at the same time. What if you then heard about the fun that others were having in the sport you did not pick or the class you did not take? You might start to second-guess yourself – to wonder if you made the right choice.

Big and small choices

Small choices – such as the colour of your school bag or which sweets to buy – are easy to forget. But what big, unforgettable decisions have you faced? Maybe you have had to give up something to help someone else. Or perhaps some choice has changed how you live your life.

If you could invent a new word for how it feels to make an important decision, what would it sound like and how would you spell it? Would the word apply to both bad and good feelings related to your choice? It is difficult to think of one word that could carry so many feelings. Perhaps this is why many writers use poems to describe their understanding of these moments. Poets – and other writers – often return to moments of choice because these are the times that come to define us. They are the moments that change our direction in life.

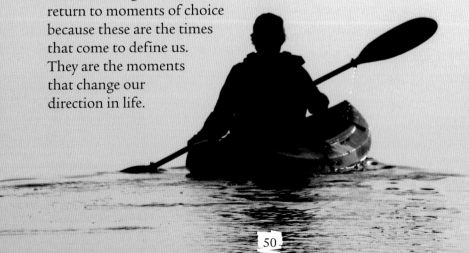

SENSE OF DIRECTION

A chart like this can help you analyse a choice or conflict in a poem, such as "The Road Not Taken". The same kind of chart can help you think about choices and conflicts in your own life.

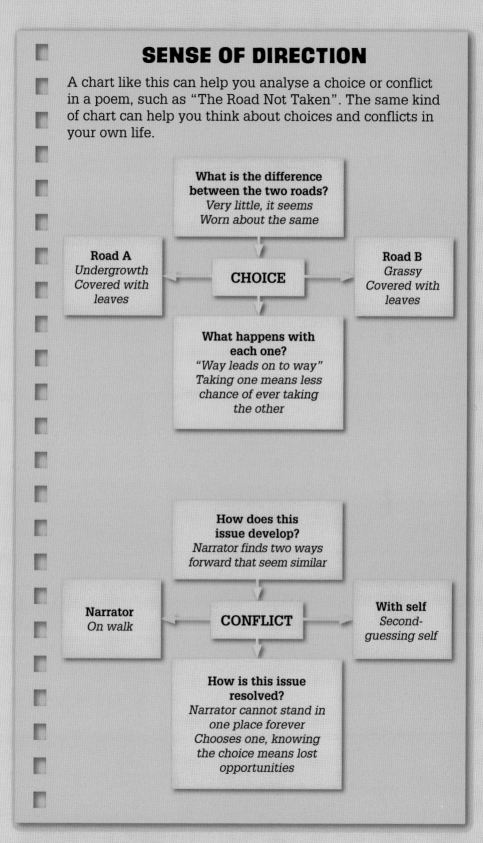

What is the difference between the two roads?
Very little, it seems
Worn about the same

Road A
Undergrowth
Covered with leaves

CHOICE

Road B
Grassy
Covered with leaves

What happens with each one?
"Way leads on to way"
Taking one means less chance of ever taking the other

How does this issue develop?
Narrator finds two ways forward that seem similar

Narrator
On walk

CONFLICT

With self
Second-guessing self

How is this issue resolved?
Narrator cannot stand in one place forever
Chooses one, knowing the choice means lost opportunities

Alternate endings

At moments of choice, we can sense the possibility of different outcomes. Yet, ready or not, we have to make a decision. We must choose the story our lives will tell. In much the same way, poets weigh different outcomes as they write. Think of Tennyson writing about the "six hundred". What if he chose to write about a soldier who ran from battle instead? What if he spoke through the officer who sent the soldiers to their deaths?

What if Trethewey's speaker chose to challenge the teacher? How might a poem about that confrontation look? What if Giovanni's narrator chose to scream at people rather than cry? With each detail, a poet decides on the tone of the message the poem will carry. It is up to the reader to find and interpret that message.

The joy of poetry

In poetry, the reader who looks for encouragement can find it; the reader who hunts for big ideas can discover them. The reader who seeks understanding can find endless possibilities. Experiencing poetry is a way to better understand what other people think and feel. So, use what you learn to help yourself and others. Just one surprising turn in a poem can make all the difference – see where it takes you!

APPROACHING A POEM

Use this checklist to review five ways that you can study a poem. The questions listed here can lead you to the poem's meaning.

Structure
- What does the poem look like as a whole? What do the stanzas and lines look like?
- Are there end rhymes or interior rhymes?
- Is there a pattern to the metre?
- What is the function of each verse or section? Does it reveal more or different information? If so, what and why?

Decide: Is this formal or open verse? How effective is it?

Facts
- Who is the speaker or narrator?
- What is happening?
- Where is the feeling or story happening?
- When is the time frame?

Decide: Why does this poem exist? What is the main idea?

Images
- Which images stand out?
- What text creates the images?
- How do the images connect with the senses (seeing, hearing, smelling, tasting, touching)?
- Are there similes, metaphors, or personifications?

Decide: Do the images allude to other ideas? Are the images effective?

Sounds
- Which sounds stand out in the text?
- What role do rhymes play?
- Does metre play a role?
- Is there alliteration, assonance, or consonance?

Decide: How do the sounds and patterns of sound help form the tone and message?

Meaning
- What denotations do the words have?
- What connotations do the words have?
- How does figurative language affect the meaning?
- How do the sounds and images affect the meaning?

Decide: How would you describe these elements of meaning?

Write your own poem about choices

There is no better way to experience poetry than to write it yourself. This collection shows what different poets have had to say about choices. Now, think about a choice that has meant something to you and share your insights on the subject.

To think about what you will say, you can begin with a warm-up exercise. Think about basic choices you have made:

- *I had five pounds, so I...*
- *The biggest choice I ever had to face was...*
- *The flavour I wanted was...*
- *Instead of...*
- *I could have kept quiet, but...*
- *I felt lost, so...*
- *I thought it was funny, so...*

Try out different ideas until one feels right to you. If you get stuck, take more time. Use a notebook to take notes about choices that you make throughout a day or a week. You can draw sketches that show what you are thinking and feeling. Collect photographs that go with your theme. When you hear lines of songs that inspire you, write them down. Allow one thought to build on another.

Staying on topic

After settling on the moment of choice you will write about, think about metaphors that work with your idea. When you consider your choice, what images come to mind? Robert Frost thought of a road that divides in a yellow wood. Mary Wroth thought of a labyrinth. What concrete images can you think of that show a choice in the making?

There is no wrong answer to questions like these. Just be confident that the details of your life are what will make your poem stand out as something fresh and new. Most people can picture a pathway in a wood. The trick is to be specific. How does Frost make you imagine this *particular* pathway?

If it helps, you can write a letter to yourself on the subject. See what ideas and images come up. To take another point of view, think about choices that have meaning to other people you know. Imagine yourself facing the choices that others have to make.

CONCEPT WEB

A concept web can help you find your way to an inspiring topic. Begin by writing a word or a few words that represent a choice you want to explore. Then, add other words and phrases that come to mind around it. Include ideas that appeal to the senses of sight, taste, touch, hearing, and smell.

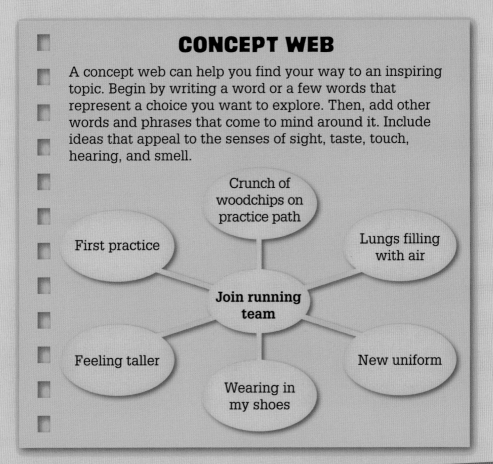

Connect to sounds and pictures

Allow the words to show up on the page without judging them. See where open verse can take you. At the start, the important thing is to connect to the images, rather than finding the perfect words. You can always go back and rework the words if necessary. As you write, you can play with the line breaks and with your choice of words. Remember that white space and punctuation are clues to stop for a moment or to slow down. Commas tell the reader to pause, and full stops say "stop and breathe".

Follow the rules

You could try to write in formal forms by following the patterns of the classic poems in this book. Or you may choose to write a poem that is a mix of both open forms and set patterns. You can try writing a **ghazal**, which features at least five pairs of lines, called couplets. Here are the rules:

- Ten or more lines come in pairs, and the first pair rhymes.
- Every line has the same number of syllables.
- The final word or words of the second line of the first couplet repeat in the second line of every pair that follows, as a refrain.
- Your name or the meaning of your name appears in the final couplet.

Student of language

Poets are lifelong students of language. The act of writing offers its own encouragement, and there is joy in getting better at saying what once seemed impossible to say. Writing becomes both work and play as you continue to study poetry. There are many more types, or genres, of poetry than are covered here. See what others you can find out about.

If you get stuck on one part, or one image, you can work out your ideas to the side. Think about the thing you want to describe. Try writing about it as if you were making instructions for how to draw it. Or try writing about it as if you were far away. Then write about it as if you were close to it. See which description lends itself to your poem.

As you write, keep reading your poem aloud. Listen for the sounds that you like. Consider why you like them. Listen for areas that you wish to improve. Remember, poets play with words!

Bibliography

The following were valuable sources of information for this book.

Books

A Dictionary of Symbols, J. E. Cirlot (Philosophical Library, 1962)

Hip-Hop Poetry and the Classics for the Classroom, Alan Sitomer and Michael Cirelli (Milk Jug Publishing, 2004)

How Does a Poem Mean?, John Ciardi (Houghton Mifflin, 1959)

Maud and Other Poems, Alfred, Lord Tennyson (Ticknor and Fields, 1855. Copy shared on Google by Harvard University Library)

Native Guard: Poems, Trethewey, Natasha (Houghton Mifflin Company, 2007)

Word Wise & Content Rich, Douglas Fisher and Nancy Frey (Heinemann, 2008)

Websites

www.emilydickinsonmuseum.org
Emily Dickinson Museum.

www.english.illinois.edu/maps/poets/g_l/haas/haiku.htm
Modern American Poets: Robert Haas on Haiku.

www.georgiaencyclopedia.org/nge/Article.jsp?id=h-3697
The New Georgia Encyclopedia: Natasha Trethewey.

www.gillianclarke.co.uk/home.htm
Gillian Clarke's website.

http://myloc.gov/Exhibitions/books-that-shaped-america/1900-1950/ExhibitObjects/New-Hampshire.aspx
Library of Congress: Books That Shaped America: Robert Frost, *New Hampshire*.

http://nikki-giovanni.com
Nikki Giovanni's website.

www.poetryfoundation.org/bio/mary-wroth
Poetry Foundation: Mary Wroth.

www.webexhibits.org/poetry/explore_21_visual_examples.html
Poetry Through the Ages: Poetry that knows no bounds.

Glossary

adjacent next to

alliteration repetition of consonant sounds at the start of words that follow one another

allusion reference to other parts of a culture, such as historical events or works of art

assonance repetition of sounds, especially vowel sounds

autobiographical from the author's life

ballad type of lyric poem meant for singing

biography story about a person's life, written by someone else

cavalry soldiers on horseback

chronological order arranged in order of the time events occurred

collaborative poem poem written by more than one person

concrete poetry poems written in shapes that suggest the subject-matter of the writing

connotation set of ideas associated with a particular word

consonance repetition of consonant sounds

context words around another word that give clues to its meaning

contradictory two or more things that disagree with or oppose each other

Cossack cavalry soldier from Ukraine or Russia

denotation official or dictionary definition of a word

end rhyme repetition of sound at the end of consecutive lines

figure of speech expression that uses language in a way different from the literal meaning of the words involved

foot unit of rhythm

ghazal form of poetry made up of rhyming couplets and a refrain, each with the same metre

haiku poem made up of 17 syllables arranged in three lines

half rhyme repetition of only the final consonant sounds in words

iambic pentameter five iambs (duh-DUH sounds) in a row

imagery figurative language that represents objects

imperfect rhyme sounds that almost rhyme

Industrial Revolution period beginning in the late 18th century, in which machines began to be widely used to make products

infer gather or conclude by reasoning from evidence

internal rhyme rhyme that occurs within lines

intrinsic part of or belonging to the nature of something

introspective deeply aware of one's own thoughts and feelings

italicize print in the kind of type that slants to the right

lexicon stock or collection of words

lyric poem musical poem expressing thoughts about emotions

metaphor figure of speech that links two things, carrying an aspect of one thing to another

metre pattern of rhythm in poems, determined by the stresses on syllables

mythology traditional stories of a people, often concerning heroes and supernatural events

narrative poem poem that tells a story

narrator speaker telling the story

near rhyme sounds that almost rhyme

open form poetry poetry that does not follow traditional patterns and structures of rhythm and rhyme

oxymoron figure of speech that shows opposite feelings at the same time

paraphrase explain the same thing using different words

parentheses curved brackets

perfect rhyme when the last syllable of two words have the same sound

persona identity that a writer assumes (the speaker)

personify give human characteristics to a non-human object or concept

plantation large farm that usually grows one type of crop

Poet Laureate official poet of a country, who writes poems for important national occasions

point of view perspective from which a story is told

prefix common group of letters at the beginning of a word

pronoun word that substitutes for a noun, such as "I", "my", "his", or "her"

prose ordinary form of writing or speech

refrain stanza that repeats

resolution the way a conflict works out

sabring using a sabre (a kind of sword)

setting place where the action or feeling occurs

simile figure of speech that compares two things using the words "like", "as", "if", or "than"

sonnet form of verse with 14 lines and a consistent pattern of rhyme

speculate wonder about, or guess at

stanza group of lines that are similar

stressed given emphasis (the opposite is "unstressed")

subterfuge deception

suffix common group of letters at the end of a word

summarize tell the main points about something in short form

survey assess something's structure

symbol something that is used to represent something else

tone writer's attitude toward the subject matter

understatement deliberately making something less obvious or seem less important than it really is

verse line of poetry or, sometimes, poetry in general

visual rhythm shape of a poem and length of its lines

Find out more

Books

Norton Anthology of Poetry, Margaret Ferguson, Mary Jo Salter, et al. (eds)
(Norton, 2004)
A go-to reference, this gigantic encyclopedia of poetry spans from
the medieval period to the present. The 5th Edition contains 1,828
poems by 334 poets, along with small introductions and biographies
for each author.

Poetry Matters: Writing a Poem from the Inside Out, Ralph Fletcher
(HarperCollins, 2002)
Want help finding ideas for poems? Looking for tools and
techniques to help develop your poems? Ralph Fletcher's book is a
guide for young writers who feel called to write poetry.

A Kick in the Head: An Everyday Guide to Poetic Forms, Paul B. Janeczko
(Candlewick, 2009)
For exploring some of the most popular forms of poetry from all
over the world (including haiku and sonnets) look no further. Paul
Janeczko covers the rules and provides great examples for 29 unique
poetic forms.

Poetry for Young People: Langston Hughes, David Roessel and Arnold
Rampersad (Sterling Children's Books, 2013)
The Poetry for Young People series explores the works of notable
poets, which includes the poems of Langston Hughes, an important
African American author who wrote about his thoughts and
experiences in the early 20th century.

Websites

www.auburn.edu/~downejm/hyperepos.html
Many classic works such as *Beowulf*, *The Iliad*, *The Odyssey*, and
Paradise Lost are considered epic poems. Here, you can find online
texts, historical contexts, bibliographies, and critical resources all
about epic poems.

http://edl.byu.edu
The website of the Emily Dickinson Lexicon, with a searchable database to explain the words used by the reclusive poet.

www.loc.gov/poetry/media/poetvision.html
The Library of Congress offers two series exploring some great American poets from the 20th and 21st centuries. *Poet Vision* is a 12-part series of interviews with famous poets such as Allen Ginsberg and Robert Penn Warren. The Poet and the Poem is an ongoing series of interviews with currently active writers.

http://poetryfoundation.org
The official website of the Poetry Foundation, which publishes *Poetry* magazine. Use their archives and resources to read selected poems, learn about prominent poets, and discover the history of different types of poetry.

http://youngpoets.org
Sponsored by the National Schools Project, the Young American Poetry Digest is one of the best publishing opportunities out there for young poets. Visit the official website to check out submission guidelines.

Acknowledgements
We would like to thank the following for permission to reproduce photographs: Corbis pp. 29 (Colin McPherson), 31 (Splash News), 33, 36 (Mimmo Jodice), 39 (Blue Lantern Studio); Dreamstime pp. 14–15 (Maryo99), 28 (Milanexpo), 35 (Vesilvio), 37 (Rnd), 41 (Elenathewise), 45 (Chepe); Flickr p. 7 (KimonBerlin); Getty pp. 11 (Time & Life Pictures), 18, 20–21, 21 (Time & Life Pictures); Library of Congress p. 46; Shutterstock pp. 5 (Artur Synenko), 6 (Teerasak), 9 (djgis), 10 (inxti), 12–13 (Vladimir Sklyarov), 16–17 (Richard Cavalleri), 24 (Netfalls - Remy Musser), 25 (Michael Cohen), 26 (Dhoxax), 27 (Smoliakov Andrii), 42 (Boudikka), 44 (ollirg), 50 (David B. Petersen), 52–53 (Pavelk), 55 (Brenda Carson), 56–57 (Pichugin Dmitry); SuperStock pp. 22–23 (Universal Images Group), 47 (Christie's Images Ltd.), 48 (Susan E. Pease/age footstock); Wikipedia: p. 43 (Brett Weinstein).

Index